HOW? WHO? WHAT? WHEN? WHERE? WHY?

Questions
kids
ask

ABOUT
STORIES AND FAIRYTALES

PUBLISHER	Joseph R. DeVarennes	
PUBLICATION DIRECTOR	Kenneth H. Pearson	
ADVISORS	Roger Aubin	
	Robert Furlonger	
EDITORIAL SUPERVISOR	Jocelyn Smyth	
PRODUCTION MANAGER	Ernest Homewood	
PRODUCTION ASSISTANTS	Martine Gingras	Kathy Kishimoto
	Catherine Gordon	Peter Thomlison
CONTRIBUTORS	Alison Dickie	Nancy Prasad
	Bill Ivy	Lois Rock
	Jacqueline Kendel	Merebeth Switzer
	Anne Langdon	Dave Taylor
	Sheila Macdonald	Alison Tharen
	Susan Marshall	Donna Thomson
	Pamela Martin	Pam Young
	Colin McCance	
SENIOR EDITOR	Robin Rivers	
EDITORS	Brian Cross	Ann Martin
	Anne Louise Mahoney	Mayta Tannenbaum
PUBLICATION ADMINISTRATOR	Anna Good	
ART AND DESIGN	Richard Comely	Ronald Migliore
	Robert B. Curry	Penelope Moir
	George Elliott	Marion Stuck
	Marilyn James	Bill Suddick
	Robert Johanssen	Sue Wilkinson

Canadian Cataloguing in Publication Data

Main entry under title:

Questions kids ask about stories and fairy tales.

(Questions kids ask ; 26)
ISBN 0-7172-2565-8

1. Fairy tales—Miscellanea—Juvenile literature.
2. Folk literature—Miscellanea—Juvenile literature.
3. Children's questions and answers.
I. Smyth, Jocelyn.   II. Comely, Richard.   III. Series.

GR550.Q48 1988   j398   C89-093175-5

Questions Kids Ask . . . about STORIES and FAIRYTALES

continued

What is a fairytale?

Have you ever wondered just what it is that turns a plain story into a fairytale? It's magic! The name fairytale is given to all stories in which wonderful things happen by magic. Jack was given magic beans in *Jack and the Beanstalk*. Dorothy wore magic ruby slippers in *The Wizard of Oz*. It was magic that turned Cinderella from a poor girl into a beautiful princess.

The moment you start to read a fairytale, you enter a magical, make-believe world where the impossible becomes possible and "once upon a time," everyone lived "happily ever after"!

5

Why do you have to be very careful when you have three wishes?

How many times a day do you make a wish? Quite a few, if you're like most people. You may wish you didn't have to get up in the morning and that you didn't have to go to school. That's two wishes already! If you had been given three wishes, you would only have one left.

The classic fairytale, *The Three Wishes,* tells how often people wish without thinking about what they're doing. There are many versions of the story. In one, a man catches a goblin who grants him three wishes. The man gives two of the wishes to his wife. During dinner, the wife, who can't get the marrow out of a bone, unthinkingly wishes that her husband had a bird's beak. The husband, furious at finding a beak on his face, immediately wishes that his wife had one, too. That's two wishes. There's only one left, and only one thing to do—use the third wish to repair the damage done by the first two.

So if someone ever gives *you* three wishes, be sure you think very carefully because whatever you wish for may come true!

Why did Scheherazade make up 1001 stories?

I like it! I like it!

The Thousand and One Nights is a collection of folktales from Arabia, India and Persia. Ali Baba, Sinbad and Aladdin appear in these stories, which were supposedly made up by Scheherazade.

The first story is Scheherazade's own. She has become the bride of a cruel king who has decided to marry a new woman each night and have her killed the next morning. But Scheherezade has a plan to outwit her new husband. She begins a long story that she doesn't have time to finish that night. The king is fascinated and allows her to live another day so she can finish it. One story leads to another, until, after 1001 nights, the king has fallen in love with her and lets her live.

DID YOU KNOW . . . one of Scheherazade's stories is that of Aladdin, a poor boy who finds a magic lamp. When he rubs the lamp, a genie, or spirit, appears to make all Aladdin's wishes come true!

How do you get to Never-Never Land?

"Second to the right," Peter said, "and then straight on till morning."

That's where Never-Never Land is, and that's where Peter Pan takes John, Wendy and Michael Darling. The children meet Tinker Bell, Captain Hook, the Lost Boys and other famous characters in the classic tale *Peter Pan*. Although the directions seem rather vague to us, the children fly directly to Never-Never Land with the help of a little fairy dust and "strange to say, they all recognised it at once."

Peter Pan is a play written by James Barrie, a British author. Barrie later rewrote the story in book form and called it *Peter Pan and Wendy*.

Why did Pinocchio's nose grow?

A woodcarver named Geppetto wanted to make a puppet that could dance and leap like an acrobat. As he was carving the puppet Pinocchio, the eyes moved and stared at him. The mouth stuck out its tongue at him. The hands snatched off his wig and the feet kicked poor Geppetto in the nose!

This was strange, considering it was just a wooden puppet. But stranger still was the fact that when Pinocchio told a lie, his nose began to grow. Once, he told so many lies that his nose kept growing until he couldn't move without hitting the bed, the window, the walls or the door!

You can read about Pinocchio in *The Adventures of Pinocchio,* by Carlo Collodi.

What is the tooth fairy?

When one of your baby teeth falls out, do you put it under your pillow when you go to bed that night? What happens to it—in the morning it is gone! But in its place is some money: 25 cents, 50 cents or maybe even more.

Your parents tell you your tooth was taken by the tooth fairy —a small supernatural being who likes to do things for humans. You have no use for your old tooth. But the tooth fairy does.

People say that in fairyland, where everything is small, the tooth fairy lines the paths to her house with white baby molars. With the sharp, front teeth she makes tiny spades and shovels to dig in her garden. And she uses the smallest, prettiest teeth to teeth to make necklaces and other pieces of fine jewelry.

It seems like a fair exchange—don't you agree?

Do fairies have a king and queen?

Fairies have been around for a long time. For hundreds of years, they have been found in stories, novels, poems and plays. Fairies are imaginary, magical creatures who exist in the folklore of almost every country in the world.

Legend says fairies live alone or in large groups in fairyland, a place where no one ever gets sick and time stands still. It is ruled by a king and queen. Queen Mab is a famous fairy queen in Irish folklore. Oberon and Titania are fairyland's king and queen in many tales. In most stories, the queen has more power than the king.

FAIRYLAND

What is a changeling?

In the old days, mothers often feared that their newborn infant would be stolen away by the fairies, who would leave a fairy child in its place. Sometimes the fairy child, or changeling, was sickly, ugly or stupid. Sometimes it was an old, worn-out fairy, who wanted to rest and be cared for.

Some say the best way to get rid of a changeling is to make it laugh.

It will disappear and the true child will appear in its place. Others say that if the changeling is well cared for, the fairy mother will be so pleased that she will bring the human baby back to its mother and give them both good luck forever.

A few stories tell of changelings growing up among mortals. Often they have some extraordinary ability—such as being able to see in the dark or to make strange, bewitching fairy music.

Does the bogeyman carry off naughty children?

Since olden times, parents have warned their children: "You'd better be good or the bogeyman will get you." Who was this mysterious bogeyman? English and Scottish legends tell of a mischievous or evil goblin called a *bogie* or *bogie beast*. He is also known as hobgoblin, bug, bogle and bogy. Always terrifyingly ugly, he may have glowing eyes as big as saucers. He can assume all sorts of horrible shapes and sometimes appears headless.

Does he carry off naughty children? Well, have any you know disappeared after being naughty? No? Maybe they started behaving (as parents hoped they would) and escaped the bogeyman's clutches. If you want to see a bogeyman, try saying:

"Bogeyman, bogeyman, can't get me"—and let us know what happens!

Who had to run as fast as she could to stay in the same place?

The next time you step through a mirror and find yourself in a strange country, look for Alice. That's what she did in a story by Lewis Carroll called *Through the Looking Glass,* and the country she found was strange indeed. There, Alice discovered, if you run as fast as you can, you stay in the same place. So how can you ever get anywhere? The Red Queen explains, "If you want to get somewhere else, you must run at least twice as fast as that!"

What was peculiar about the Cheshire Cat?

We all know that when cats are happy, they purr. But have you ever seen a cat smile?

In Lewis Carroll's story *Alice's Adventures in Wonderland,* the Cheshire Cat does just that. Even Alice, who has met many weird and wonderful creatures during her travels, is surprised to see the cat grin from ear to ear.

When the Cheshire Cat vanishes, its grin is the last thing to disappear. This leads Alice to remark: "Well! I've often seen a cat without a grin, but a grin without a cat! It's the most curious thing I ever saw in all my life!"

Who was Mother Goose?

Mother Goose is an imaginary little old lady who was supposed to have created the popular children's nursery rhymes and stories. Some people believe that she was a real person whose name was Elizabeth Vergoose, and that she made up the songs, rhymes and stories for her grandchildren. However, there is no proof that this is true.

Mother Goose was probably not a real person. Many of the rhymes she is given credit for writing existed hundreds of years before they were called Mother Goose rhymes. The name Mother Goose was most likely invented by a Frenchman named Charles Perrault. In 1697 Perrault published *Contes de ma Mère l'Oye* (Tales of Mother Goose). This was the first time that the name Mother Goose appeared in print.

What was the first fairytale collection?

The oldest known collection of fairytales is the *Panchatantra* (the Five Tantars or Books). This Hindu collection dates back to the third century. English readers know it as *Fables of Bidpai*. The collection contains early versions of such fairytales as *The Three Wishes* and *Puss in Boots*. These are still popular today!

Who was the Pied Piper of Hamelin?

As legend has it, the villagers of Hamelin in Germany offered a traveling magician a large sum of money to get rid of the rats that had infested their town. The magician—the Pied Piper—took up a set of magic pipes and began to play strange music that lured all the rats out of hiding and into the Weser River where they drowned. When the piper returned to collect his reward, however, the townspeople refused to pay him. Angry, he took up his pipes again and this time enchanted the children of Hamelin. He led them, so the story goes, into Koppenberg Hill where they disappeared, never to be seen again.

Scholars are convinced that the story is based on a real event, but they have not found a way to prove what the event was or who was the real life model for the Pied Piper.

Are all goblins mean?

You've probably heard tales of goblins coming out of fairyland, especially on Hallowe'en, to play tricks on people. Legend says that goblins are the meanest and ugliest kind of fairy. Sometimes they appear in the shape of animals, and they are the thieves and villains of fairyland.

But not all goblins are totally evil. There are certain goblins that are said to live in mines in England. They are called knockers because they make knocking sounds to lead miners to the best sources of metals. Knockers are generally friendly, but they can't resist the odd trick. Sometimes they pull their already ugly face into even more horrible shapes while performing grotesque dances. They don't like whistling, so miners who whistle have a shower of pebbles thrown on their head if a knocker hears them. To keep a knocker happy, English folktales say miners must leave a small part of their lunch for the goblins to gobble.

When did knights live?

The wonderful adventures of King Arthur and his knights of the Round Table were stories of courage and honor. But being a knight wasn't always considered a great honor.

The word *knight* comes from an Old English word meaning servant. In England around 1066, any man could be a knight. Many lords had knights who were servants in peacetime and soldiers in wartime.

About 100 years later, knights became a class of their own, and received honor and distinction. During the Middle Ages, between 1100 and 1300, English knights fought for their lords, and competed in jousting tournaments. This period was called the Age of Chivalry, after the strict code of behavior the knights observed.

When gunpowder and guns became war weapons, they replaced the knight's sword and dagger on the battlefield. Today in England, knighthood is a ceremonial honor given to reward outstanding public service.

Who was Gulliver?

Gulliver is the hero of a book called *Gulliver's Travels,* written over 250 years ago by Jonathan Swift. He is a ship's surgeon and he has an amazing series of adventures.

First, he is shipwrecked and finds himself washed up on the shore of Lilliput, a land whose inhabitants are so tiny he can hold them in his hand. Next, Gulliver is accidentally left in Brobdingnag, a country where everyone is as tall as a house, snobbish and nasty.

The original *Gulliver's Travels* was meant for adults, to expose their follies and vices. Eventually, someone produced a shorter, simpler version that has become a favorite with children everywhere.

Who was Humpty Dumpty?

Eggs are a popular folklore theme because they represent the beginning of life. The most famous egg character is Humpty Dumpty, the star of an old riddle rhyme that has many versions.

Almost every European country claims to have had the original of Humpty Dumpty. But the likeliest claim is that Humpty was actually based on King Charles I of England and a war machine that was supposed to win him the civil war.

Charles was a very short man and like Humpty he had small, weak legs. The war machine was nicknamed "Humpty Dumpty" because it was designed to "hump" down the hill and "dump" the rebel army off their horses. Unfortunately for Charles, Humpty Dumpty fell off the wall and broke while crashing down the hill. The king's army couldn't save it—or the king. Charles was defeated and fled England in 1642.

DID YOU KNOW . . . Humpty Dumpty appears with Alice in Lewis Carroll's novel, *Through the Looking Glass*.

What is a gremlin?

Have you ever seen something that looked like a cross between a jack-rabbit and a bull terrier, and wore green breeches, a red jacket, a top hat and spats? That's a gremlin.

Gremlins are imaginary creatures who cause mechanical problems in airplanes. It is thought gremlins were invented by British pilots during World War I, but they became most famous during World War II. When anything went wrong on a plane, the crew would say, "It must be a gremlin."

According to legend, gremlins are fond of drinking gasoline, distracting the pilot, and interfering with radio communications. You wouldn't want to have a gremlin aboard on your next flight—it could mean trouble!

Who is the strongest girl in the world?

What would you do if you lived all alone, didn't have to go to school, and could buy 16 kilograms (35 pounds) of candy at a time?

That's how Pippi Longstocking lives. Not only that, Pippi is the strongest girl in the world. She can even lift her pet horse onto the roof of her house! Police officers can't stop her. She simply picks them up and carries them to the curb.

The larger-than-life character Pippi Longstocking was created by Swedish author Astrid Lindgren in the 1950s.

DID YOU KNOW . . . when Pippi makes cookies, she rolls the dough out on her kitchen floor!

What are leprechauns?

The Irish have their own breed of fairies, called leprechauns. These tiny men are usually under a metre (3 feet) tall and dress all in green. Many are believed to have a hidden stash of gold. Legend has it that to have good luck you must see a leprechaun before he sees you and disappears.

Most leprechauns are merry, hardworking shoemakers, but they enjoy playing tricks on people. According to one story, a farmer caught a leprechaun in his field and made him reveal where his gold was buried. The leprechaun pointed at a particular plant. The farmer tied his red hanky to the plant to mark it, and went home for a shovel. The leprechaun knew just how to trick the farmer, who returned to find every plant in the field tied with a red hanky!

What happened to everything Midas touched?

Midas, a king in ancient Greece, did a kind deed for one of the gods. As a reward, he was granted one wish. Midas loved gold, so without stopping to think, he asked that whatever he touch turn to gold.

Midas picked up a twig to test his new power. Instantly it turned to gold. He picked up a stone and it too became gold. Midas was overjoyed and ordered a great feast to celebrate.

He sat at the table laden with food, and reached for the bread. But he couldn't eat—it had turned to gold. The wine touched his lips and became liquid gold. Midas was miserable. His daughter, whom he loved dearly, tried to comfort him and became a golden statue in his arms. Midas wept and begged the god to take away his golden touch. The god took pity and let Midas wash away the gift in a special river.

Who was "Little Jack Horner"?

Little Jack Horner
Sat in the corner,
Eating his Christmas pie;
He stuck in his thumb,
And pulled out a plum,
And said, "What a good
boy am I."

There's an interesting story behind this nursery rhyme.

In the time of King Henry VIII of England, there lived a man called John, also known as Jack, Horner. His job was to take messages to the king. A favorite trick at the time was to hide important papers in pies. One day Jack was sent to London with a pie for the king. Baked into it were the title deeds for several estates. Jack Horner pulled a fast one. *He stuck in his thumb*—into the pie—and stole the king's *plum*—the land deed for a choice property.

Perhaps Jack Horner then had to be nimble and quick, in order to get away before the angry king caught him!

What kind of rabbit is the Easter bunny?

In many countries, it's a childhood belief that the Easter bunny brings colored eggs and candy for children to find.

Like many modern customs, this one comes from ancient beliefs. And according to these beliefs, the Easter bunny isn't a bunny, it's a hare!

In the legends of ancient Egypt, the hare was associated with springtime because it was the symbol of fertility and the beginning of new life. After Christianity was born, it became a tradition to celebrate Easter in the spring. The ancient symbol of springtime, the hare, thus became associated with Easter.

Since most people can't tell the difference between a rabbit and a hare, the symbol of the hare became commonly known as the Easter bunny. Exactly what kind of hare it is, isn't known. The Easter bunny could be a snowshoe hare or an Arctic hare or even a jackrabbit—which, by the way, is a hare in spite of its name.

Who is Captain Nemo?

Captain Nemo is a character in the novel *Twenty Thousand Leagues Under the Sea* by Jules Verne, one of the pioneers of science fiction. In the novel, Professor Arronax sets sail to investigate mysterious attacks on ships at sea. His own ship is attacked and sunk, and he is rescued by the *Nautilus,* a strange vessel that can sail under the ocean. It is commanded by the mysterious Captain Nemo, who has been been sinking the ships of nations he blames for harming his nation. Eventually, Captain Nemo regrets taking the lives of so many people, and destroys the *Nautilus*—and himself.

Where is Narnia?

You won't find Narnia on any map of the known world. That's because Narnia exists in the world of imagination. It's a magical land found in a series of books by C.S. Lewis.

Narnia is an enchanted valley created by Aslan, a great lion. There are dwarves and centaurs there, and wood spirits and unicorns, mermaids, mermen, castles, caves, a dancing lawn and an evil White Witch.

You can get to Narnia through the back of a wardrobe made of wood from a magical Narnian apple tree. Or through the Wood Between the Worlds, using magic rings to transport you. But if Narnia is in danger and Aslan needs you, he will use his power to take you there directly, and send you home the same way!

Who's afraid of the Big Bad Wolf?

You are, if you're like the two silly pigs in the classic English fairytale, *Three Little Pigs.* You're afraid that he'll huff and he'll puff and he'll blow your house down.

In 1933, Walt Disney made this story into the most popular cartoon short ever. It was a smash hit and received a lot of publicity. Even though the entire film was less than ten minutes long, people lined up for blocks to see it. Part of its popularity was due to its theme song, ''Who's Afraid of the Big Bad Wolf?'' written by composer Frank E. Churchill. The song became one of the biggest radio hits of the year. It was the first time a cartoon had ever created a hit song.

Do all countries have fairytales?

In a German fairytale, a girl named Ashputtel can't go to a ball because her stepmother makes her pick lentils out of the ashes. An old Filipino story tells of a girl named Maria who can't go to the ball because she has to wash clothes in the river. Both girls make it to the ball with the help of magic and eventually marry the handsome prince.

Sound familiar? We know the girl as Cinderella, but almost every country in the world has its own version of the same story.

No one knows for certain where this story began. It has been carried from country to country, told and retold by thousands of different people who each added something to it. In many places, the same story with a different twist became part of that country's folklore.

Folktales later formed the basis of what we now call fairytales. All countries have them, and the fairytales of one country often resemble those of another.

Index